SALZBURG

Christmas Vacation Guide
2024/2025

A Complete Pocket Guide to Festive Markets,
Top Attractions & Snowy Adventures in
Austria's Winter Wonderland

Wendy T. Sierra

Copyright

All rights reserved. No part of this publication may be reproduced, distributed, or transmitted in any form or by any means, including photocopying, recording, or other electronic or mechanical methods, without the prior written permission of the owner.

©[2024][Wendy T. Sierra]

Table of Contents

Copyright..........1
Table of Contents..........2
Forward.......... 3
Introduction..........5
Arriving in Salzburg.......... 11
Accommodation Guide.......... 17
Salzburg's Iconic Christmas Markets..........26
Must-See Christmas Attractions..........34
Hidden Winter Gems in Salzburg..........43
Salzburg Christmas Concerts & Events.......... 50
Best Winter Outdoor Activities.......... 57
Christmas Dining in Salzburg.......... 63
Family-Friendly Christmas Experiences........ 69
Shopping for Christmas Gifts..........75
Day Trips From Salzburg..........81
Sustainable & Eco-Friendly Winter Travel..... 87
Salzburg Christmas Traditions & Folklore..... 93
Practical Tips for Your Christmas Vacation... 99
Conclusion.......... 105

Forward

Welcome to your journey through the enchanting world of **Salzburg at Christmas**. As you flip through these pages, you are about to step into a place where centuries-old traditions blend seamlessly with the joy and magic of the festive season. Nestled in the heart of the Austrian Alps, Salzburg transforms into a winter wonderland every December, its cobblestone streets, historic squares, and grand baroque architecture glowing under twinkling lights and a blanket of snow.

Christmas in Salzburg is more than just a holiday; it's an experience steeped in history, culture, and the spirit of togetherness. Here, you'll find something for everyone—whether you're drawn to the warmth of cozy cafés serving Austrian pastries or the excitement of bustling Christmas markets filled with local handicrafts and holiday treats. For those seeking adventure, Salzburg's surrounding snow-capped mountains offer thrilling outdoor activities like skiing, tobogganing, and ice skating. And for the music lovers, what could be better than spending Christmas in the birthplace of Mozart, with the sound of classical concerts filling the air?

This guide is designed to be your companion as you discover Salzburg's most beloved Christmas traditions, its hidden gems, and the many ways in which the city comes to life during the holidays. Each chapter will lead you through its charming streets, offering insights into the best places to visit, where to stay, and how to fully immerse yourself in the festive spirit.

Whether you're a first-time visitor or someone who has already fallen in love with Salzburg, this book will help you make the most of your Christmas vacation. From practical tips on navigating the city in winter to insider advice on must-see events and attractions, every detail has been thoughtfully curated to enhance your experience.

So, wrap yourself in your warmest scarf, sip on a cup of hot *Glühwein*, and let Salzburg's Christmas magic unfold before your eyes. We hope this guide inspires you to embrace the festive season with open arms and to create unforgettable memories in this truly magical city. Welcome to Salzburg at Christmas—it's going to be a holiday you'll never forget.

Introduction

Salzburg is a winter wonderland that feels like something out of a fairytale. The air is chilly, with the aroma of freshly baked gingerbread and mulled wine, while snow-covered rooftops glitter under strings of golden lights. As you walk down cobblestone streets, the warm glow of lanterns illuminates your path and the sounds of carolers fill the air. Salzburg seems tailor-made for Christmas, with each corner exuding charm, warmth, and a festive vibe that wraps around you like a comforting blanket.

This is a place where the joy of the holiday season is not merely felt, but lived, in every market stall, festive music, and cup of steaming hot chocolate drunk by a crackling fireplace. Whether you are a first-time visitor or someone who returns to Salzburg year after year, the city's Christmas spirit never fades. Let's look at what makes Salzburg one of the world's most wonderful Christmas destinations.

Overview of Salzburg's Winter Wonderland

When the first snowflakes fall in Salzburg, the city transforms into a beautiful winter paradise. Salzburg's exquisite baroque buildings, set against the backdrop of the majestic Alps, are even more stunning when snow falls. As the chilly air sharpens, the city comes alive with festive decorations, twinkling lights, and the ringing of Christmas bells in the streets.

This makeover is centered on Salzburg's old town, which retains its historic beauty. Walking through the small roads, you'll notice storefront displays adorned with Christmas wreaths, glittering ornaments, and beautiful snow globes. Domplatz und Residenzplatz, the city's principal squares, host lively Christmas markets. The aroma of roasted chestnuts, spiced wine, and sweet pastries wafts through the air, beckoning tourists to linger and enjoy the season.

The thrill of Salzburg's winter wonderland lies not just in its beauty, but also in the experience. Ice skating at Mozartplatz, sledding down mild slopes, or simply exploring the festive streets wrapped in your warmest scarf all make for unforgettable experiences. The entire city feels like a living snow globe.

Christmas Atmosphere and Festivities

The mood in Salzburg at Christmas is nothing short of spectacular. Every year, the city celebrates its centuries-old traditions with both elegance and joy. Whether it's the dazzling lights dotting the streets or the sound of church bells resounding from Salzburg Cathedral, the holiday season here evokes both nostalgia and celebration. Here are a few highlights of the city's joyful atmosphere:

Salzburg's Christmas Markets: The Christkindlmarkt, which takes place in Domplatz and Residenzplatz, is one of Europe's oldest and most attractive Christmas markets. As you walk through its quaint wooden stalls, you'll see local artisans selling handcrafted jewelry, woolen scarves, and aromatic candles. It's the ideal place to find a one-of-a-kind present or relax with a warm mug of Glühwein while watching the world go by.

Advent Singing & Concert: Music permeates the air during the holiday season. Christmas concerts highlight Salzburg's rich musical tradition, ranging from modest choir performances in local churches to major musicals at the Mozarteum. The sound of angelic voices singing traditional songs can give anyone shivers.

The Krampus Parade: For a bit of Christmas excitement, don't miss the Krampuslauf, a centuries-old custom in which scary, masked figures parade through the streets. This unusual blend of the macabre and the joyous is a Salzburg custom that adds a dash of fascinating folklore to the Christmas season.

The Silent Night Chapel, located just outside of Salzburg, honors the birthplace of one of the world's most famous Christmas carols, "Silent Night." Visiting the church and hearing this beloved song performed in its original setting is an incredible experience.

Why Salzburg for a Christmas Vacation?

With so many lovely European cities enjoying Christmas, you may ask what makes Salzburg stand out. But once you arrive, the reasons become evident.

A Timeless Charm: Salzburg is a city that proudly wears its history, and this is especially visible during the Christmas season. Its baroque architecture, small medieval lanes, and great churches are decked out in holiday glory. The entire city feels like you're traveling back in time, where traditions are upheld and the joy of Christmas is cherished as it has for decades. Whether you're sipping mulled wine at a centuries-old market or seeing a symphony in a medieval auditorium, Salzburg's ageless appeal is obvious.

Musical Heritage: Few places can match Salzburg's musical legacy. As Mozart's birthplace, the city has music in its DNA. This tradition is celebrated during Christmas with wonderful concerts ranging from classical to soulful carols. Salzburg is the quintessential Christmas destination for music lovers, with every note encapsulating the season's joy and magic.

Breathtaking Scenery: With the Alps as a backdrop, Salzburg's natural beauty is undeniable. In the winter, the snow-capped mountains provide a dramatic touch to the city's landscape. Whether you're looking out over the city from Hohensalzburg Fortress or enjoying a day trip to the surrounding countryside, Salzburg's winter environment is breathtaking.

Festive Spirit in Every Corner: In Salzburg, Christmas is more than just a holiday; it is a season of festivity. From late November to December, the city's festive energy is contagious. Every square, street corner, every business exudes holiday cheer. It is hard to stroll through Salzburg without experiencing the warmth and excitement of Christmas.

Salzburg during Christmas is a beautiful combination of history, music, and festivities. Whether you're attracted by its beautiful markets, rich musical traditions, or simply the romanticism of a snow-covered city, Salzburg is the ideal place for a holiday season filled with surprise and delight.

Arriving in Salzburg

Salzburg is one of Europe's most popular holiday destinations, and getting there is easy, whether by air, train, or vehicle. However, the winter weather and the surge of travelers during the holiday season can make travel difficult if you are not prepared. This section offers a helpful guide on arriving in Salzburg and navigating around the city during the Christmas season.

Best Travel Routes to Salzburg

Salzburg's center location in Europe allows for easy access from a variety of important cities. Here are the best ways to get to Salzburg based on your starting point.

By Air: The quickest and most convenient method to get to Salzburg from abroad is to fly into **Salzburg Airport W.A. Mozart (SZG).** This modest but well-connected airport is only 4 kilometers from the city center, and during the winter season, several airlines fly straight from major European cities such as London, Berlin, Paris, and Amsterdam.

- **From the Airport to the City:** Taxis and buses provide convenient transportation from the airport to the city center. The O-Bus Line 10 runs every ten minutes and takes around 20 minutes to get to the heart of Salzburg. Taxis are also easily accessible, charging between €15 and €20 for a trip into the city center.

By Train: Train travel is a convenient and scenic choice for individuals going from other regions of Europe, particularly from surrounding countries such as Germany, Austria, or Switzerland. Salzburgs Hauptbahnhof (Main Train Station) is well-connected with major cities such as Vienna, Munich, and Zurich.

- **Vienna to Salzburg:** The high-speed Railjet trains run frequently and take about 2.5 hours.
- **Munich to Salzburg:** The rail travel takes 1.5 hours and there are direct trains every hour.

The trains are generally reliable, although during the winter season, it's a good idea to buy tickets ahead of time, especially around Christmas, when trains tend to fill up rapidly.

By Car: Driving to Salzburg is an excellent choice for those seeking flexibility. The city is well connected to major highways. It takes roughly 1.5 hours to get from Munich via the **A8 motorway**. The **A1 motorway** journey from Vienna takes approximately 3 hours. It's worth noting that Austrian law requires cars to have winter tires from November to April, and snow chains are a smart idea if you plan on driving in high terrain.

- **Parking in Salzburg:** Parking in the city center can be scarce, particularly during the peak vacation season. There are various public parking facilities, although it is generally more convenient to park at your hotel or use park-and-ride services on the outskirts of town.

Getting Around Salzburg inWinter

Once you've arrived in Salzburg, moving around is rather simple, even in the winter. The city's compact size makes it easy to walk about, but for cold days or longer travels, there are various public transportation choices.

Walking: The old center of Salzburg is modest and easily accessible by foot. The majority of the city's main attractions, like the Christmas markets, Hohensalzburg Fortress, and Mozart's Birthplace, are easily accessible by foot. Wear warm clothing and good-grip shoes in the winter, as the cobblestone streets can be slick after snowfall.

Public Transportation: Salzburg's public transportation system is efficient, with buses and trolleybuses (O-Bus) running frequently around the city. The Salzburg Card is a convenient choice for travelers, providing unlimited public transportation and free admission to many of the city's attractions. It is available for 24, 48, or 72 hours and can be purchased via tourist information centers or online.

- **Buses:** Salzburg's bus network connects the majority of the city, including important tourist attractions and Christmas markets. Buses run often, however schedules may change during holidays.
- **Taxis:** Taxis are easily available in Salzburg, especially near the main rail station and airport. However, at peak

occasions such as Christmas Eve and New Year's, it can be more difficult to find a cab promptly, so prepare ahead if you require one.

Cycling: Salzburg offers a comprehensive network of bike routes for individuals who enjoy cycling. While winter cycling may not be for everyone, the city nonetheless maintains several of its bike lanes during the colder months. Rental bikes are available, however cycling may not be the greatest option in snowy or slippery conditions.

Transportation Tips for the Festive Season

Traveling during the Christmas season in Salzburg can be enjoyable, but it is crucial to plan ahead of time due to increased visitor numbers and the possibility of winter weather problems. Here are some ideas to ensure smooth travel:

Book in advance: The holiday season is one of the busiest times of year in Salzburg, whether it's for flights, rail tickets, or accommodations. Booking early gives you the finest alternatives and can often save you money.

Prepare for winter weather: Salzburg has cold and snowy winters, so pack accordingly. Dress in layers, pack a thick coat, hat, and gloves, and wear shoes designed for walking on snow or ice. Weather conditions might also have an impact on travel plans, so it's a good idea to check them on a frequent basis.

Use public Transportation: While driving is allowed in Salzburg, the public transit system is fast and user-friendly, particularly during the busy Christmas season when parking can be difficult to locate. To get around the city, use the bus, a taxi, or walk.

Holiday Hours: During the Christmas season, many shops, restaurants, and even public transportation services operate on reduced hours, especially on Christmas Eve and Day. Make sure to check the opening timings and transportation arrangements in advance.

Accommodation Guide

Finding the ideal spot to stay during your Christmas break in Salzburg will substantially improve your whole experience. Whether you choose a magnificent hotel with views of snow-capped mountains, a quaint boutique with festive décor, or a low-cost stay that nonetheless provides warmth and comfort, Salzburg has it all. In this chapter, we'll take you through some of the best accommodations to make your Christmas stay as comfortable and wonderful as the city itself.

Top Hotels and Inns for a Cozy Christmas Stay

If your ideal Christmas vacation includes staying somewhere luxurious yet cozy, Salzburg has a variety of top-tier hotels and inns. These lodgings mix comfort and festive elegance, providing a warm and inviting respite after a day spent enjoying the city's Christmas markets and winter scenery.

Hotel Sacher Salzburg: Hotel Sacher, one of Salzburg's most prominent hotels, is noted for combining traditional elegance with modern conveniences. During the Christmas season, the hotel is tastefully adorned, creating the ideal backdrop for a warm yet sophisticated visit. The hotel, located on the banks of the Salzach River, provides spectacular views of the Old Town, which is especially magical when covered with snow.

- **Why it's perfect for Christmas:** The hotel serves a delicious Christmas Eve meal and traditional Austrian delights such as Sachertorte (renowned chocolate cake). The exquisite decor, combined with the celebratory atmosphere, provides for an unforgettable visit.

Hotel Goldener Hirsch: Hotel Goldener Hirsch provides a one-of-a-kind blend of 600 years of history and modern elegance for visitors seeking a historic stay. This hotel is located on Getreidegasse, one of Salzburg's main retail districts, and is just a few feet from several of the city's finest Christmas attractions. The hotel's small rooms, designed in typical Alpine style, offer warmth and charm.

- **Why it's perfect for Christmas:** This hotel's cozy environment and rustic charm make it the ideal place to unwind after browsing the Christmas markets. The hotel's restaurant serves delectable Austrian cuisine, and the lovely fireplace in the lounge is perfect for warming up after a winter stroll.

Hotel Schloss Mönchstein: If you want to invest in a memorable Christmas experience, Hotel Schloss Mönchstein is a luxury castle hotel set on a mountaintop with breathtaking views of Salzburg. The hotel's compact size and customized care provide a warm, exclusive ambiance, and during the holidays, it feels like you're vacationing in your own winter castle.

- **Why it's Excellent for Christmas:** With its storybook location, this hotel is ideal for a romantic or family Christmas holiday. Its spa is great for relaxing after a day of sightseeing, and the castle's Christmas decorations add to the enchanting atmosphere.

Boutique Hotels with a Festive Flair

Salzburg's boutique hotels cater to individuals who seek smaller, more intimate rooms with a festive flare. These hotels are often located in or near the historic district, making them ideal for soaking up the city's Christmas spirit.

Arthotel Blaue Gans: Housed in a historic building on Getreidegasse, Arthotel Blaue Gans blends modern design with a joyful and welcoming ambiance. The hotel's blend of contemporary art and traditional features gives it a distinct personality, and it's gorgeously decorated for the holiday season.

- **Why it's Excellent for Christmas:** With only 35 rooms, the hotel provides a cozy and intimate atmosphere. The festive décor and proximity to the Christmas markets make it an excellent choice for visitors who want to be in the center of the activity while staying in style.

Hotel and Villa Auersperg: A family-run boutique hotel, Hotel Auersperg provides a welcoming and personalized experience, especially during the holiday season. Located just outside the city center, it provides a calm getaway while remaining within walking distance of Salzburg's main attractions.

- **Why it's wonderful for Christmas:** During the holiday season, the hotel's garden is converted into a winter wonderland, and the snug lounge with a fireplace is the ideal place to unwind with a warm drink after a day in the cold. The personalized treatment and meticulous attention to detail make it feel like a home away from home.

Budget-Friendly Christmas Stays

Traveling on a budget does not need you to lose out on Salzburg's Christmas charm. The city has a wide range of cheap lodgings that provide comfort and festive spirit without breaking the bank.

MEININGER Hotel Salzburg City Center: MEININGER Hotel is an excellent choice for guests looking for low-cost accommodation without sacrificing comfort. Even during the busiest holiday season, this modern, clean, and conveniently situated hotel offers reasonable rates.

- **Why it's perfect for Christmas:** With cozy rooms and a shared kitchen, this hotel is ideal for families or parties vacationing together. Its position, just a short bus ride from the city center, makes it convenient to see Salzburg's Christmas markets and festive festivities.

Hotel Imlauer and Bräu: Hotel Imlauer & Bräu is located near Salzburg's major train station and offers nice rooms at a reasonable price. The hotel's typical Austrian style creates a warm atmosphere, and its location is ideal for exploring the city center and local attractions.

- **Why it's ideal for Christmas:** The hotel provides a festive environment at affordable rates. The hotel's restaurant serves traditional Austrian cuisine, so you can enjoy a hearty meal before heading out to the Christmas markets.

Yoho International Youth Hostel: This Youth Hostel is a great option for budget-conscious guests. This hostel, located within walking distance of the city center, provides both private and dormitory-style accommodations at reasonable prices.

- **Why it's perfect for Christmas:** The hostel's welcoming environment and communal facilities make it simple to meet other tourists. Furthermore, its position makes it easy to enjoy Salzburg's festive offerings without overspending on lodging.

Family Friendly Accommodations

If you're traveling with children, selecting the correct lodging is essential for a pleasant and pleasurable vacation. Fortunately, Salzburg has lots of family-friendly options that meet the demands of families while maintaining a lively atmosphere.

Radisson Blu Hotel Altstadt: This centrally located hotel has big family rooms and a warm atmosphere for families. The Radisson Blu

Hotel Altstadt is adjacent to many of Salzburg's finest Christmas sights, making it convenient to explore the city with children.

- **Why it's ideal for families:** With its spacious rooms and central location, families can simply walk to surrounding Christmas markets and return to the hotel for rest. The hotel also provides babysitting services, allowing parents to spend a relaxing evening.

Hotel Garni Frauenschuh: Hotel Garni Frauenschuh is located in a calmer area of Salzburg and provides larger family suites as well as a peaceful, child-friendly setting. The hotel features a playground and is only a short drive from the city center, making it an ideal location for families.

- **Why it's Excellent 1 for families:** The big accommodations, outdoor areas, and family-friendly service make it an excellent choice for parents traveling with children. Furthermore, the hotel's warm and welcoming environment is ideal for making unforgettable Christmas memories with your family.

Salzburg offers a magnificent environment for your Christmas vacation, regardless of your budget or travel style. From deluxe hotels to low-cost hostels, you'll be able to locate a comfortable location to stay during your holiday vacation.

Salzburg's Iconic Christmas Markets

Being in Salzburg during Christmas is like stepping into a winter fantasy, with festive lights adorning every part of the city, snow covering the rooftops, and the aroma of roasted chestnuts filling the air. One of the most fascinating aspects of Salzburg's holiday season is its well-known Christmas markets, where locals and visitors alike congregate to buy unique gifts, sip mulled wine, and soak up the festive mood.

The city's Christmas markets are a spectacular blend of history, tradition, and holiday spirit. From the centuries-old Christkindlmarkt on Domplatz to the enchanting Hellbrunner

26

Adventzauber at Hellbrunn Palace, each market has its own distinct appeal. Let us tour Salzburg's most famous Christmas markets and the delights that await you!

Christkindlmarkt at Domplatz and Residenzplatz

The Christkindlmarkt at Domplatz and Residenzplatz, one of the world's oldest and most famous Christmas markets, is a must-see for any Christmas visitor to Salzburg. Located in the center of the city's Old Town, this market has been a tradition for over 500 years, making it one of Austria's most popular holiday destinations.

Atmosphere: With the towering Salzburg Cathedral as a backdrop, the Christkindlmarkt is reminiscent of a Christmas novel. The market's dazzling lights and festive decorations create a wonderful ambiance, with carolers singing traditional Austrian Christmas songs and the aroma of spiced punch filling the air.

What to Expect: As you walk through the market's rows of wooden stalls, you'll come across a treasure trove of handcrafted ornaments, nativity sets, and locally made presents. From delicate glass-blown ornaments to hand-carved wooden sculptures, each piece tells a tale about Salzburg's rich artisanal history. Make sure to try local specialties like Lebkuchen (gingerbread cookies) and the famed **Bosna sausages**. And, of course, no visit is complete without a mug of Glühwein, a hot mulled wine that will keep you warm while you peruse the market's festive delights.

Special Highlights: Don't miss the ceremonial lighting of the Christmas tree in the market's center, which is a towering beauty covered with brilliant lights and decorations. The Christkindlmarkt also features performances by local choirs and brass bands, filling the air with the sound of festive pleasure.

Hellbrunner Adventzauber: The Magic of Hellbrunn Palace

The Hellbrunner Adventzauber, or "Advent Magic of **Hellbrunn Palace**," is a short drive from the city center and offers a genuinely spectacular Christmas market experience. Set against the breathtaking backdrop of Hellbrunn Palace, the market transforms the palace grounds into a winter paradise that appears almost too magical to be true.

Atmosphere: Imagine walking through a courtyard filled with 700 lighted Christmas trees, with the palace lighting softly in the background. The Hellbrunner Adventzauber is one of Salzburg's most family-friendly markets, with a fun atmosphere and stunning decorations. Children can enjoy a petting zoo, pony rides, and perhaps meet Santa Claus himself.

What to Expect: Unlike the crowded Christkindlmarkt, this market has a more calm, private atmosphere. You'll find a beautiful range of artisanal goods, like hand-knitted scarves and traditional Austrian sweets. If you're traveling with children, they'll enjoy the palace's outdoor advent calendar, which opens each window one by one during the Advent season.

Special Features: One of the market's biggest attractions is the Hellbrunner Christmas Path, a magnificently lit walkway that snakes through the palace's gardens, transporting guests on a fantastic journey via shimmering trees and seasonal installations. If you want to warm up, visit one of the pleasant fire pits sprinkled throughout the market, where you can sip hot chocolate and roast marshmallows.

Stern Advent Market at Sternbräu

For a more hidden treasure experience, head to the Stern Advent Market, which is set in the charming courtyards of the historic Sternbräu Brewery. Tucked away from the main tourist attractions, this market has a quieter, more intimate atmosphere with plenty of holiday charm.

Atmosphere: The atmosphere at the Stern Advent Market is that of a private Christmas retreat. The tiny courtyards are decked with fairy lights, and the market's small size lends it a friendly, neighborly atmosphere. It's the ideal place to escape the crowds and spend a relaxing evening with friends and family.

What to Expect: The Stern Advent Market is recognized for showcasing local handicrafts and tasty foods. You'll find vendors offering exquisitely produced pottery, jewelry, and textiles created by local craftsmen. The food vendors are a highlight, with everything from classic Austrian sweets to excellent cheese-filled pretzels. For beer aficionados, don't miss out on sampling some of the Sternbräu Brewery's seasonal brews.

Mirabelle Square Christmas Market

Another must-see during your Christmas vacation in Salzburg is the Mirabell Square Christmas Market, which is located in the gardens of the famed Mirabell Palace. Mirabell Square, while smaller than some of the other markets, provides a quiet, relaxed ambiance in which to enjoy the festive spirit without the clamor and bustle of larger people.

Atmosphere: The market is placed against the picturesque backdrop of Mirabell royal, with the royal grounds offering a calm respite from the bustling city center. During the evening, the market is attractively illuminated, and you can enjoy breathtaking views of Salzburg's Old Town and surrounding fortress.

What to Expect: Despite its tiny size, this market has an excellent range of holiday presents, such as handmade candles, woolen goods, and traditional Christmas decorations. You'll also find a variety of delectable goodies, including hot roasted chestnuts and freshly baked pretzels. This market's modest size makes it ideal for a leisurely stroll, especially if you prefer a quieter, more relaxed atmosphere.

Unique Local Handicrafts and Delicacies

One of the most enjoyable aspects of Salzburg's Christmas markets is the opportunity to discover distinctive local handicrafts and cuisine. Whether you're seeking a unique gift to take home or simply want to immerse yourself in local culture, the markets include a diverse assortment of objects reflecting Salzburg's artistic past.

Handmade Ornaments: Many kiosks sell finely created decorations made of glass, wood, or ceramic. These decorations, which range from fragile glass angels to meticulously carved nativity scenes, are ideal for decorating your tree and make great gifts.

Austrian Woolen Goods: Traditional Austrian knitwear is a popular item at the markets. From soft woolen scarves to hand-knit socks, these comfortable accessories will keep you warm on your winter adventures.

Local Delicacies: The food at Salzburg's Christmas markets is not to be missed. Enjoy regional favorites such as **Kaiserschmarrn** (fluffy shredded pancakes), **Käsespätzle** (cheese noodles), and **Bauernkrapfen** (Austrian doughnuts). If you pair your goodies with a steaming mug of Glühwein or hot chocolate, you'll have the perfect winter snack!

Salzburg's Christmas markets are more than just a shopping destination; they celebrate the city's rich traditions, festive spirit, and community love. Whether you're hunting for the perfect present, trying some local specialties, or simply taking in the lovely atmosphere, these markets are sure to make your heart sing with festive cheer. Happy Christmas shopping!

Must-See Christmas Attractions

When you stroll through Salzburg during the winter, it seems as though the city has been transformed into a living snow globe. It's impossible not to feel amazed and nostalgic as snowflakes gently fall from the sky and dust the cobblestone streets and rooftops. The combination of Christmas cheer, Baroque architecture, and Salzburg's rich history create an atmosphere that feels timeless and takes you back to bygone eras.

The famous sites of Salzburg take on a whole new charm when you tour the city during the holidays. Salzburg's historic monuments are drenched in the charm of the season, from the imposing **Hohensalzburg Fortress**, standing vigil over the city, to the exquisite **Mirabell Palace and Gardens** converted into a winter paradise. Let's explore this enchanted city's must-see Christmas attractions.

Hohensalzburg Fortress in Winter

The Hohensalzburg Fortress, perched high above Salzburg's skyline, is a tribute to the city's enduring vitality and a reminder of its medieval past. With its towers blanketed in snow and its stunning views of the city below, a visit to the fortress in the winter seems like entering a fairy tale. The Hohensalzburg Fortress, the largest fully preserved fortress in Central Europe, is a must-see not only for its historical value but also for its breathtaking winter splendor.

Atmosphere: You'll be treated to expansive vistas of Salzburg covered in snow as you ascend to the fortress, either by funicular or on foot. The white walls of the stronghold contrast sharply with the surrounding wintry scenery, making it an impressive picture. The castle's interior rooms and courtyards are replete with artifacts from its time in the Middle Ages to its use in the city's defense.

What to Do: Go on a guided tour of the fortress's magnificent chambers to learn about the archbishops who formerly presided over Salzburg and the fortress's involvement in several wars throughout the ages. Don't miss the **Chapel of St. George,** a tiny but exquisitely preserved Gothic chapel, or the Golden Hall, an extravagant space decorated with gold leaf and detailed woodwork. Following your tour, ascend to the **viewing platform** for sweeping views of Salzburg's Old Town, the Salzach River, and the distant, snow-capped Alps.

Mirabell Palace and Gardens with Winter Charm

A beloved feature of Salzburg's environment, the graceful Mirabell Palace and Gardens acquire a unique beauty throughout the winter months. The formal gardens, which are so colorful in the summer, are turned into a tranquil winter wonderland with snow covering the immaculately trimmed hedges and statues. The magnificent Baroque architecture of Mirabell Palace itself serves as a reminder of Salzburg's regal heritage.

Atmosphere: The atmosphere In the winter, strolling around the Mirabell Gardens is a serene, almost surreal experience. With the backdrop of snow-covered woods, the statues appear to come to life, the walks are peaceful, and the fountains are frozen over. The symmetrical design of the gardens creates a lovely view from every angle, and the eccentric stone sculptures in the **Dwarf Garden** seem especially charming when surrounded by snow.

What to Do: Spend some time exploring the Marble Hall inside Mirabell Palace, which was formerly the venue for opulent court parties. These days, it's well-known for holding classical performances featuring the sounds of Mozart, the most well-known son of Salzburg. After that, take a stroll around the grounds and take in the subdued beauty of the wintry scenery. During the holidays, the fortress and cathedral can be seen from the gardens in an especially lovely setting.

The Magic of Mozartplatz During Christmas

Mozartplatz, named after **Wolfgang Amadeus Mozart**, the most well-known citizen of the city, is located in the center of Salzburg's Old Town. This square is transformed into one of Salzburg's most enchanting locations during the holiday season by the jolly sound of Christmas songs, sparkling lights, and festive decorations. With the snow gently falling all around him, the imposing monument of Mozart stands proudly in the middle of the square, presiding over the festivities.

Atmosphere: The atmosphere of Mozartplatz, a center of holiday activity, is characterized by market booths offering delectable Austrian sweets, mulled wine, and handcrafted crafts. The lively mood is enhanced by the adjoining Christkindlmarkt, which overflows into the square. You can feel the festive atmosphere permeating the square as you stroll about, from the exquisitely decorated Christmas trees to the sounds of local musicians performing Mozart compositions.

What to Do: Pay homage to Salzburg's greatest composer by taking a moment to observe the Mozart Statue, which was built in 1842. After that, browse the surrounding vendors for anything from traditional **Lebkuchen** (gingerbread) to handcrafted ornaments. If you're lucky, you might be able to see one of the live events held in the square throughout the Advent season. These events include choirs singing traditional Austrian carols and brass bands performing.

39

DomQuartier: Salzburg Cathedral & Winter Exhibits

One of Salzburg's most significant cultural icons, the **DomQuartier** is particularly alluring at Christmas. This historic complex offers a tour through Salzburg's artistic and religious past and houses the Salzburg Cathedral, the **Residenz**, and other museums. During the holiday season, the magnificent **Salzburg Cathedral**, with its breathtaking Baroque grandeur, is an especially poignant location to visit, especially during the **Christmas services** when the cathedral is filled with the sound of prayer and singing.

Atmosphere: The atmosphere Wintertime at the DomQuartier is like traveling back in time. A sight to behold is the majestic façade of the cathedral, framed by the snow-covered mountains. The cathedral's magnificent interior, with its soaring ceilings and elaborate decorations, is even more breathtaking when lit up for the holidays.

What to Do: Visit the museums in the **DomQuartier** to see the amazing collection of religious items and art. Don't miss seeing the archbishops of Salzburg's tombs in the **cathedral's crypt**. After that, stroll around the **Residenz**, the former archbishops' palace, to see the opulent state chambers and discover more about Salzburg's past as a political center.

Mozart's Birthplace: A Historic Christmas Visit

One of Salzburg's most treasured landmarks, Mozart's Birthplace, is a must-see when visiting the city. Wolfgang Amadeus Mozart was born in this humble yellow building on Getreidegasse in 1756. The museum has a nostalgic charm during the Christmas season as people flock there to honor the composer who revolutionized the music industry.

Atmosphere: The atmosphere Entering Mozart's Birthplace will take you back in time to the eighteenth century. Original manuscripts, musical instruments, and personal belongings are among the museum's exhibits that provide insight into Mozart's early years and the environment he lived in. The structure itself gives off the impression that not much has changed since Mozart's day, with its small staircases and groaning wooden floors.

What to Do: Learn about Mozart's family, his early musical training, and his ascent to fame by embarking on a self-guided tour of the museum. Christmastime at the museum is especially moving because local musicians and performers fill the streets with the sounds of Mozart's compositions. After your visit, stroll down **Getreidegasse**; the holiday décor and glistening lights will transport you back to a bygone era of Christmas.

The well-known Christmas attractions in Salzburg enable visitors a deeper connection to the city's jolly customs and rich history in addition to being breathtaking sights. Every location is infused with the romance and nostalgia of Christmas, whether you're seeing a medieval stronghold, meandering through Baroque mansions, or going to the birthplace of one of the greatest composers in history. These encounters will not only leave you in awe but also engulf you in the coziness and magic of the season, making your Salzburg Christmas genuinely remarkable.

Hidden Winter Gems in Salzburg

In the shadows of Salzburg's busy Christmas markets and great sights, quiet places and age-old customs await those with a sense of wonder. The city's hidden winter pearls provide more than simply stunning vistas and seasonal happiness; they inspire you to go off the usual route and discover the city's hidden, sometimes unnoticed, beauties.

There's something magical about coming upon a snow-covered route that seems undisturbed by time, or discovering a local ritual that appears to whisper tales about Salzburg's history. The beautiful city's secret nooks are shrouded in a festive shroud, ready to display their enchantment. From tranquil winter walks to the warm embrace of a secret café, these encounters will take you deep into Salzburg's quiet mysteries.

Peaceful Winter Walks in St. Peter's Cemetery

During the winter, the gently falling snow produces a covering of tranquil beauty, imbuing St. Peter's Cemetery with a feeling of serenity and timelessness. This historic cemetery, one of Salzburg's oldest, transforms into a peaceful haven away from the city's festive frenzy, giving an atmosphere of introspection. St. Peter's, also known as Petersfriedhof, is more than simply a memorial to Salzburg's glorious history; it's a hidden jewel nestled among the imposing cliffs of Mönchsberg, waiting for visitors seeking quiet amid the Christmas bustle.

Atmosphere: Wandering around the cemetery's small walkways, you'll come across snow-dusted gravestones, their inscriptions fading with time, each one a quiet testament to Salzburg's long and storied past. The modest, well maintained graves are covered with Christmas wreaths, candles, and flowers left by loved ones, providing warmth to the winter environment. Overhead, the cliffside catacombs, etched into the rock, serve as a cryptic reminder of Salzburg's ancient roots.

What to Do: Take a leisurely stroll around the cemetery, allowing yourself to absorb the history around you. Pause beside the tomb of Johann Michael Haydn, the renowned composer's brother, and ponder on the musical legacy ingrained in this hallowed land. As you walk past the old graves and crypts, the calm is both spooky and lovely, a tranquil respite in the midst of the festive season. For those who love a little intrigue, try visiting the catacombs, which provide a unique view of the cemetery below.

The Secret Christmas Traditions of Mülln

Mülln, located on the outskirts of Salzburg's Old Town, is a neighborhood rich in history and local folklore. While visitors throng to the bigger Christmas markets, Müllners observe their own quieter, more hidden traditions throughout the holiday season. Here, centuries-old traditions merge with the winter scenery, creating an ambiance that is both fascinating and mysterious.

Atmosphere: The meandering lanes of Mülln are lined with snow-covered buildings, their windows beaming with warm, golden light. As you travel around the neighborhood, you'll find little nativity scenes that have been meticulously handcrafted and set on windowsills or outside courtyards, each telling a unique narrative. Müllners have long cherished the tradition of "**Anklöpfeln**," a medieval Christmas ceremony in which groups of singers travel door to door, singing ancient songs and bestowing blessings.

What to Do: If you're lucky enough to visit Mülln in the evening, listen for the sound of carolers quietly singing as they pass from home to house. These acts are not for show; they are deeply ingrained in the local community, and watching one feels like learning a long-held secret. After your stroll, visit **Müllner Bräu**, a historic brewery where you may warm yourself with a local beer or a hot cup of mulled wine, which is a popular winter custom in this hidden part of Salzburg.

Winter Serenity at Leopoldskron Palace

While many tourists to Salzburg are attracted to the grandeur of the Hohensalzburg Fortress or the festive ambiance of Mirabell Gardens, the peaceful beauty of Leopoldskron Palace is often overlooked. This Baroque mansion, placed against the background of the frozen Leopoldskroner Weiher lake, creates a winter landscape so exquisite that it seems like entering a dream. During the Christmas season, the royal grounds remain calm, providing a serene respite from the city's busier attractions.

Atmosphere: As you approach the castle, the towering mountains in the background and the snow-covered trees create a scene of pure winter splendor. The frozen lake reflects the palace's magnificent façade, producing an image right out of a Christmas card. The quiet waterways, now solid with ice, encourage skaters and nature lovers alike to enjoy the peacefulness that winter offers to this ancient estate.

What to Do: Take a leisurely walk around the lake, pausing to observe the palace's reflections and the surrounding countryside. For a really magnificent experience, go around sunset, when the final light of day gives a golden glow on the snow and the castle seems to shimmer in the fading light. If you're fortunate, you could see some locals skating on the lake, which is a popular winter activity in Salzburg. After your stroll, warm up at Schloss Leopoldskron, where the palace's comfortable café serves festive snacks and provides a lovely view of the surrounding winter scenery.

Hidden Cafés For Festive Treats and Hot Chocolate
Salzburg's busy Christmas markets are packed with food booths selling every type of holiday

delight conceivable, but for those looking for a calmer, cozier environment, the city's secret cafés are the ideal escape. Tucked away on little side alleys or hidden behind unassuming doors, these cafés give more than simply a place to rest—they are a haven of warmth and pleasure in the middle of winter's harshness.

Atmosphere: Stepping inside one of Salzburg's secret cafés seems like entering a world apart from the bustling streets outside. The perfume of freshly made Apfelstrudel permeates the air, blending with the rich aromas of hot chocolate and mulled wine. The darkly lighted rooms, filled with seasonal decorations, provide a friendly, intimate environment in which time seems to slow down.

What to do: Visit **Café Tomaselli,** one of Salzburg's oldest and most popular cafés. You may enjoy classic Austrian pastries while observing the snowfall via the huge windows. For those with a sweet craving, Café Fürst is a hidden treasure famed for its handcrafted **Mozartkugeln,** which are delectable chocolate and marzipan confections named after Salzburg's most famous native. Wherever you decide to stay, be sure to get a steaming cup of hot chocolate topped with a large swirl of whipped cream, the ideal accompaniment to a quiet moment of introspection in Salzburg's festive embrace.

Salzburg's secret winter jewels provide a look into the city's more peaceful, mysterious side. Whether you're wandering through a snow-covered graveyard, learning about hidden local rituals, or sipping a hot drink in a secluded café, these experiences will transport you further into Salzburg's winter charm. Away from the masses, you'll discover the genuine heart of this city, enveloped in the tranquility and enchantment of the season.

Salzburg Christmas Concerts & Events

Salzburg, the city of song, never seems more alive with sound and joy than during the holiday season. As the snow slowly falls on the ancient roofs and the streets glimmer with holiday lights, Mozart's melodies, timeless carols, and traditional songs fill the crisp air, creating a magical mood. Attending a holiday concert or play in Salzburg is about more than simply hearing the music; it's about experiencing the enchantment of Christmas in every note, harmony, and resonant chord.

Salzburg's musical offerings range from large opera buildings to small candle-lit churches, reflecting the city's rich cultural legacy and profound love of all things festive. Whether you enjoy classical music, traditional carols, or just admire the beauty of live performance, Salzburg's Christmas concerts and activities are sure to touch your spirit and enrich your holiday experience.

Traditional Christmas Concerts & Choir Performances

During the Christmas season, Salzburg's magnificent cathedrals and concert halls are filled with the sounds of traditional carols and holy music performed by world-class artists and local choirs. These performances provide a look into the heart of Salzburg's festive mood, blending the city's old-world charm with the music's eternal beauty.

Atmosphere: Imagine yourself seated in a centuries-old church, the vaulted ceilings rising above you, and the soothing glow of candles flickering on the stone walls. The weather is sharp and chilly, yet the music warms you like a nice blanket. As the choir starts to sing, their voices swell in perfect accord, infusing the room with a feeling of calm and respect. This is the essence of a Salzburg Christmas concert—an experience that goes beyond time and place, transporting you to the heart of the festive season.

What To Expect: Many Salzburg churches, notably the spectacular Salzburg Cathedral and the tiny **St. Peter's Abbey,** organize annual Christmas performances with music by **Handel, Bach,** and **Mozart.** These concerts often feature well-known songs like "Silent Night" (which originated in neighboring Oberndorf), as well as more recent works that capture the spirit of Christmas. One standout is the **Salzburg Advent Choir,** whose ethereal vocals offer a really enchanting experience, ideal for anyone looking for a moment of introspection and pleasure throughout the holiday season.

Festival Opera and Classical Music Events

For opera and classical music fans, Salzburg has a variety of festive performances that will fascinate and inspire. As Wolfgang Amadeus Mozart's birthplace, the city takes great delight in exhibiting his compositions, particularly around the holiday season. However, you'll also discover a broad range of different musical genres, from large operatic performances to exquisite chamber music, all suffused with holiday joy.

Atmosphere: Attending a classical performance or opera in Salzburg during the Christmas season is definitely elegant. The grandeur of the **Salzburg State Theatre** or the beautiful **Mozarteum** produces a feeling of occasion, with visitors dressed to the nines, and the air thick with expectancy and excitement. As soon as the orchestra plays its first note, the music flows through the crowd like a wave, taking with it everything of the Christmas season's pleasure, drama, and beauty.

What to Expect: During the winter months, the **Salzburg State Theatre** often produces festive operas, such as **Mozart's "The Magic Flute**," while the **Mozarteum Orchestra** presents a series of Christmas performances that combine classical classics with cheerful tunes. These activities are ideal for anyone wanting to experience the full grandeur of Salzburg's musical tradition while also enjoying the festive ambiance of the season. Book your tickets early, as these shows are very popular with both residents and tourists.

Mozart Week: Special Winter Performances

While most people identify Mozart Week with January, this globally recognized event often starts in late December, giving visitors the opportunity to see exceptional winter concerts honoring Salzburg's most famous composer. If you happen to be in town around this period, you should definitely go to one of these concerts.

Atmosphere: Imagine sitting in the sumptuous Great Hall of the Mozarteum, surrounded by shimmering chandeliers and gilded décor, while the orchestra prepares to play a symphony composed by Salzburg's genius himself. The feeling of history is apparent, and once the music starts, you can't help but feel a strong connection to the city and its rich musical tradition. Mozart Week celebrates everything that makes Salzburg distinctive, and attending one of its performances is a genuinely unforgettable experience.

What to Expect: During Mozart Week, world-class musicians commit their lives to learning Mozart's compositions, performing anything from huge symphonies to small piano recitals. In addition to typical performances, unique events are often held that dive into Mozart's life and times, providing insights into the composer's world and his continuing effect on music today. If you like classical music, Mozart Week is a highlight of Salzburg's winter season.

Salzburg Advent Singing Tradition

One of Salzburg's most treasured holiday traditions is the **Advent Singing**, a series of joyful performances conducted in the weeks before Christmas. These performances, based on the city's folk traditions, mix music, storytelling, and poetry to create a heartfelt Advent celebration. The **Salzburger Adventsingen**, hosted at the **Großes Festspielhaus**, is the most well-known of these events, drawing guests from all over the globe.

Atmosphere: Advent Singing has a homey feel that is both nostalgic and emotionally affecting. The scene is often prepared with simple but magnificent decorations that evoke a classic Alpine Christmas, complete with snow-covered landscapes and flickering lamps. As the musicians begin to play and the singers lift their voices in song, a feeling of community pervades the room—a shared celebration of the season's pleasures, hopes, and mysteries.

What to Expect: Advent Singing often includes a combination of traditional folk music, Christmas songs, and storytelling, with a focus on the nativity narrative or themes of love, peace, and goodwill. The actors, clothed in classic Austrian garb, create a genuine and passionate environment that appeals to audiences of all ages. For many people, attending an Advent Singing event is a treasured family tradition handed down through generations to mark the start of the Christmas season.

Salzburg's Christmas concerts and festivals provide a diverse range of musical experiences, each celebrating the city's cultural legacy and festive mood. Whether you're listening to the haunting beauty of a choir in a candle-lit cathedral, savoring the grandeur of an opera, or participating in the cherished tradition of Advent Singing, Salzburg's Christmas music will be a memorable aspect of your holiday experience. Allow the songs to lead you through the season, filling your heart with pleasure, wonder, and celebration.

Best Winter Outdoor Activities

Salzburg in the winter is more than simply lovely Christmas markets and charming performances; it's also a playground for outdoor enthusiasts willing to brave the weather and have some real fun! Whether you're gliding smoothly over the ice, strolling through snowy paths, or hurtling down a toboggan track, Salzburg is a winter paradise of excitement for everyone. Grab your warmest clothes, buckle up your boots, and prepare for some high-energy, heart-pounding winter activities in and around Salzburg!

Ice Skating at Mozartplatz and Volksgarten

What could be more lovely than whirling about on ice while surrounded by the historic beauty of Salzburg's old town or the festive lights of a Winter Park? Ice skating is a traditional winter pastime that offers a unique sense of delight, and Salzburg has two ideal locations: Mozartplatz and Volksgarten.

Mozartplatz Ice Rink: With the towering Hohensalzburg Fortress and the baroque magnificence of the Old Town as backdrops, skating at Mozartplatz seems like stepping into a snow world. The rink is modest, but the mood is unforgettable, with dazzling lights, holiday music, and the scent of warm glühwein filling the air. Whether you're showing off your figure skating skills or clinging to the handrail for dear life, you'll feel the beauty of Salzburg all around.

Volksgarten Ice Rink: For those who want a wider skating area (or just want to escape the tourist hordes), Volksgarten is the place to go. During the winter, this wide park changes into an ice skating paradise, complete with a big rink where you can really pick up speed. The cheerful and energetic atmosphere at Volksgarten makes it ideal for families, groups of friends, and even single skaters looking to glide through the fresh winter air. Furthermore, music is often used to establish the atmosphere, making each loop around the rink seem like a party on Ice.

Winter Hikes and Nature Trails Around Salzburg

Salzburg's snow-draped landscapes provide an abundance of chances for winter treks for people who enjoy their winter activities to be both peaceful and adventurous. The routes lead you through woods, to stunning vistas, and along tranquil rivers, each providing a unique perspective on the splendor of winter in the Austrian Alps.

Kapuzinerberg: One of the greatest locations to begin is Kapuzinerberg, a wooded hill that towers above the city. It's a modest trek, but the rewards are enormous: panoramic views of Salzburg's cityscape, including the castle, cathedral, and snow-covered Alps in the distance. As you walk through the silent, snow-covered roads, you will be fascinated by the tranquility of the winter forest. Don't be shocked if you see a deer or two along the road; they're common in this region!

Gaisberg: If you're searching for a more challenging hike, visit **Gaisberg**, one of Salzburg's nearby mountains. In the winter, Gaisberg becomes a center for outdoor sports like skiing and paragliding, but hikers will find multiple snow-covered pathways winding up the mountain, affording breathtaking views of Salzburg and beyond. It's a workout, but once you reach the summit, you'll feel on top of the world—literally.

Sledding and Tobogganing Adventures

If you've never felt the pure delight of flying down a snow-covered hill on a sled or toboggan, Salzburg is the place to alter that! Whether you're a child or a kid at heart, sledding is one of the most exciting ways to enjoy the winter months. Salzburg boasts lots of snowy slopes and routes ideal for sledding activities.

Untersberg Toboggan Run: Untersberg, located only a short distance from Salzburg, has one of the most amazing toboggan tracks in the vicinity. The 2.5-kilometer-long course descends down the mountainside, featuring twists, turns, and heart-pounding drops that will have you smiling (and even shouting) all the way down. You may hire a sled at the top, climb on it, and let gravity do the rest. It's an exhilarating ride, and once you get to the bottom, you can warm yourself with a hot drink before heading back up for another round.

Schloss Hellbrunn Gardens: offers a more family-friendly sledding experience. The moderate slopes around the castle are ideal for a more casual sledding excursion, and the picturesque surroundings provide a magical touch to the experience. When you're finished, you may wander the gorgeous castle grounds and see the festive decorations.

Skiing Day Trips from Salzburg

Austria is well-known for its skiing, and Salzburg is conveniently positioned to take advantage of some of the country's top slopes. Whether you're a seasoned expert or a total novice, there are plenty of local ski slopes to suit all ability levels.

Ski Amadé: The Ski Amadé area, located about an hour's drive from Salzburg, is a winter sports enthusiast's heaven. This extensive network of ski resorts has hundreds of kilometers of slopes, ranging from beginner-friendly runs to difficult black diamonds for expert skiers. With cutting-edge lifts, comfortable mountain huts for après-ski, and spectacular alpine vistas, a day trip to Ski Amadé is a must-do for anybody visiting Salzburg during the winter.

Flachau: If you're searching for a family-friendly ski resort, Flachau is a great choice. Flachau, located approximately 70 kilometers from Salzburg, is part of the Ski Amadé area but has a more relaxed ambiance and lots of large, easy-to-navigate slopes ideal for novices and children. The resort also has ski courses and rentals, so don't be concerned if you're new to the sport—you'll be carving your way down the mountain in no time!

Zell am See-Kaprun: is another wonderful skiing location that is around 90 minutes from Salzburg. This location is recognized for its beautiful lakeside environment, but in the winter, it changes into a snowy wonderland with slopes for all ability levels. The **Kitzsteinhorn Glacier** ensures snow even early in the season, making it a dependable destination for skiing, snowboarding, and other winter sports.

From skating in the heart of Salzburg's historic town to skiing down world-class slopes only a short drive away, there are limitless outdoor pleasures in Salzburg throughout the winter. Whether you want an adrenaline-pumping thrill or a tranquil retreat into nature, Salzburg has the ideal mix of outdoor activities to make your winter trip memorable. So wrap up, go outdoors, and let the winter charm of Salzburg take you away!

Christmas Dining in Salzburg

Salzburg's Christmas celebrations are certainly spectacular, and the festive eating scene is a big part of it. As the winter frost sets in, the city's culinary traditions come to life, serving substantial meals, soothing pastries, and warm beverages to heal both body and spirit. Whether you're eating traditional Austrian Christmas foods, relishing pastries in a warm café, or drinking mulled wine at a lively market, the aromas of Salzburg over the holidays are simply enticing.

Traditional Christmas Dishes To Try

The holidays in Salzburg revolve on comfort food—rich, savory foods that warm you from the inside out. Austrian food shines around Christmas, with dishes handed down through generations finding their way to festive tables across the city. If you're visiting Salzburg around this time, these classic Christmas meals are a must-try.

Weihnachtsgans ("Christmas Goose"): Many Austrian Christmas meals have roasted geese as the centerpiece. Crispy on the exterior and delicate on the inside, it is traditionally served with red cabbage and potato dumplings, resulting in a symphony of savory and somewhat sweet tastes. The richness of the geese, along with the tanginess of the cabbage, is the ideal winter pleasure.

Wiener Schnitzel: While schnitzel is popular all year round, it takes on particular importance during the Christmas season. Many households cook this well-known breaded and fried veal or pig meal on Christmas Eve. With lingonberry sauce and parsley potatoes, it's a comfortable dish that never fails to please.

Karpfen (Carp): Carp is a traditional Christmas Eve dish in Austria as part of the *Feast of the Seven Fishes*. Whether roasted, fried, or poached, this delicate fish is commonly served with a creamy potato salad and a light cucumber-dill vinaigrette. The meal has a basic elegance that shows the region's commitment to long-standing traditions.

Top Restaurants For a Festive Feast

Salzburg's dining scene is well-known for its traditional Austrian cuisine, and many restaurants celebrate the holiday season with special menus. If you want to have a spectacular Christmas feast, these best restaurants will not disappoint.

St. Peter Siftskeller: St. Peter Stiftskeller, Europe's oldest restaurant, is a must-see for anyone seeking an authentic and historic eating experience. The centuries-old setting, decked with seasonal decorations, is the ideal environment for enjoying Christmas staples such as roasted goose, venison, and dumplings. The lighted setting lends a romantic touch to your supper, making it a warm and delicious experience.

Goldener Hirsch: Located in the heart of Salzburg's Old Town, this Michelin-starred restaurant inside the **Hotel Goldener Hirsch** is known for its premium Austrian cuisine. Their holiday menu often includes hearty, savory meals such as venison stew, wild game terrine, and, of course, a flawlessly roasted Christmas goose. The environment, with its classic wooden interiors, seems like entering an alpine lodge, giving warmth and comfort throughout the cold winter months.

Sternbräu: A more relaxed but nevertheless celebratory event, **Sternbräu** is a favorite option among both residents and tourists. Their menu features Austrian comfort cuisine, including Christmas classics like thick soups, schnitzel, and handmade sausages. Sternbräu's outdoor dining area turns into a winter wonderland during the holidays, with sparkling lights and heaters to keep you warm as you dine.

Cozy Cafés for Austrian Christmas Pastries

Salzburg's famed pastries are a must-try for every Christmas dining experience. During the frigid winter months, the quaint cafés dispersed across the city transform into havens of warmth, serving sweet delights that are both festive and tasty.

Apfelstrudel: No trip to Salzburg is complete without a piece of apfelstrudel. This renowned treat, composed of layers of flaky pastry filled with spiced apples and raisins, is a Christmas staple. Served warm with a dusting of powdered sugar and a dollop of whipped cream or vanilla sauce, it's the ideal way to enjoy the season's tastes.

Vanillekipferl: These crescent-shaped vanilla biscuits are traditional Austrian Christmas treats. Made with crushed almonds or hazelnuts and powdered sugar, they melt in your lips with each mouthful. They may be found in every café and bakery, usually served with a steaming cup of coffee or hot chocolate.

Sachertorte is a sumptuous chocolate cake filled with apricot jam and topped with dark chocolate glaze. Its rich, moist texture and combination of sweet and tart tastes make it an opulent treat ideal for the holidays.

Warming up with Glühwein and Other Christmas Drinks

The frigid winter air in Salzburg almost begs a warm drink in hand, and the city's markets and cafés provide precisely what you need to stay warm. Here are the beverages you should try this holiday season, ranging from conventional mulled wine to unusual local delicacies.

Glühwein: Glühwein, a spiced mulled wine, is the traditional Christmas drink in Austria. Glühwein, made from red wine, cinnamon, cloves, and oranges, is served hot in decorative mugs during the city's Christmas markets. Its sweet, warming aromas are ideal for drinking while strolling around the booths, soaking in the sights and sounds of Salzburg's winter festivities.

Punsch: For those seeking a stronger alternative to glühwein, **Punsch** is a popular choice. This hot punch combines rum, brandy, or schnapps with fruit juices and spices. It's a punchy drink (pun intended) that's popular during outdoor events.

Heiße Schokolade: If you don't drink alcohol or prefer something sweet, **heiße schokolade** (hot chocolate) is a winter must-have. Made with rich, melted chocolate and topped with whipped cream, it's the ideal drink to enjoy when snuggling up in a café or taking in the festive ambiance of the Christmas markets.

Salzburg's Christmas eating scene caters to all of the senses, with substantial meals, delicious delights, and warming beverages. Whether you're enjoying classic cuisine at a historic restaurant, indulging in pastries at a quiet café, or drinking glühwein at the markets, every meal during the Christmas season is a celebration of comfort, tradition, and indulgence.

Family-Friendly Christmas Experiences

Salzburg during Christmas is like walking into a novel, when beautiful moments are brought to life for the whole family. Twinkling lights, icy adventures, and festive joy make this city the ideal winter playground for both children and adults. Whether you're discovering animal worlds at Salzburg Zoo or seeing kids create festive masterpieces at Christmas workshops, there's no lack of fun. So wrap up the kids, throw on those mittens, and prepare for some family-friendly Christmas happiness!

Fun at Salzburg Zoo in Winter

What could be more fun for young explorers than seeing their favorite animals play in the snow? Salzburg Zoo transforms into a winter paradise, with even the animals seeming to enjoy the holiday season. With over 1,200 animals to see, ranging from cuddly alpacas to formidable lions, the zoo provides unlimited entertainment.

Winter Animal Encounters: As the temperature drops, many animals, particularly cold-weather species such as lynxes and arctic wolves, emerge to play in the fresh air. The sight of these huge creatures stalking across the snowy terrain is breathtaking, and youngsters will enjoy observing them in their natural winter environment.

Night Lantern Walks: Do you want to have an extra-special experience? During the Christmas season, the zoo conducts enchanting evening lantern walks, which allow families to explore the grounds beneath the stars while led by the soothing light of lanterns. Children will be thrilled by the holiday ambiance as they go around the zoo, wrapped up and wide-eyed.

Christmas Workshops for Kids
If your young elves like being crafts, Salzburg's Christmas workshops are ideal for them to unleash their creativity! These exciting, hands-on activities are created with children in mind, allowing them to produce festive decorations, bake holiday delights, and even manufacture their own Christmas presents.

Gingerbread Decorating: Allow the youngsters to express their inner pastry chef by decorating gingerbread cookies with multicolored icing, sprinkles and edible glitter. Many workshops across the city offer gingerbread lessons where children may create their own tasty creations. What is the best part? They may either take their masterpieces home or eat them right now if they can't stop themselves from nibbling.

Christmas Ornament Making: Special craft sessions allow youngsters to create their own Christmas decorations, ranging from sparkling baubles to hand-painted snowmen. Their imaginations will run wild as they experiment with various materials such as felt, wood, and glitter. What was the result? Unique souvenirs to adorn the family Christmas tree year after year, remembering them of their lovely Salzburg Christmas.

Festive Baking Classes: If your children like getting dirty in the kitchen, enroll them in a baking class where they may make Austrian Christmas specialties such as **Vanillekipferl** (vanilla crescent cookies) and **Linzer Augen** (jam-filled biscuits). They'll learn to measure, mix, and roll while having a great time. The warm, sweet fragrances that permeate the kitchen are guaranteed to get everyone in the Christmas mood.

Family-Friendly Christmas Markets

Salzburg's Christmas markets aren't just for adults! These festive bazaars are a utopia for children, complete with dazzling lights, happy music, and a variety of exciting activities intended just for them.

Christkindlmarkt am Residenzplatz: This is one of Salzburg's biggest and best-known markets, and it's ideal for families. The market has kid-friendly entertainment, such as puppet performances and live storytelling sessions. Stalls are brimming with delicious goodies like roasted chestnuts and chocolate-covered fruit, and children may meet Christkind (the Christmas Angel) and participate in holiday games. Don't forget to take a family picture in front of the enormous, shimmering Christmas tree!

Hellbrunner Adventzauber: At the Hellbrunn Palace Christmas market, the whole family can enjoy the palace grounds, which have been converted into a magnificent fantasy with dazzling lights and festive vendors. The children will enjoy the "Christmas Post Office," where they may write messages to Christkind or St. Nicholas. There's also a petting zoo where children can meet friendly goats and ponies—the ideal way to get into the Christmas mood.

Ice Rinks and Winter Playgrounds

What's a Christmas holiday without some snowtime activities? Salzburg's winter playgrounds and ice rinks allow families to glide, slide, and play in a snowy paradise.

Mozartplatz Ice Rink: The ice rink at Mozartplatz, located right in the middle of Salzburg's historic city, is a must-see for families. Surrounded by gorgeous buildings and Christmas decorations, this outdoor rink is a wonderful place to lace up your skates. Children may whirl and spin as their parents enjoy the festive ambiance (or participate in the skating fun!). There's also a hot chocolate station nearby to help you warm up after your skate excursion.

Volksgarten Ice Rink: For a more extensive ice skating experience, go over to Volksgarten. This expansive ice rink has plenty of area for both beginners and expert skaters. It also includes cute penguin-shaped skating aids for children who are still learning how to glide around the ice. After they've perfected their movements, treat the family to some Krapfen (Austrian doughnuts) at the neighboring café.

Winter Playgrounds: If skating isn't your thing, Salzburg's parks turn into snowy playgrounds for winter entertainment. Families may construct snowmen, engage in snowball battles, or just take a picturesque stroll across the snowy terrain. Some parks even have toboggan slopes where children may go down on sleds while giggling the whole way.

Salzburg is brimming with family-friendly Christmas activities, ranging from snow-covered animal expeditions to festive craft projects. Every area of the city is packed with festive enjoyment, resulting in unforgettable experiences that your family will remember for years. So collect the kids, wrap them in scarves and hats, and prepare for a holiday filled with laughter, pleasure, and amazing Christmas memories.

Shopping for Christmas Gifts

When it comes to Christmas shopping, Salzburg turns into a festive wonderland, brimming with glittering markets, quaint shops, and one-of-a-kind finds. Imagine walking through snow-dusted streets, the aroma of roasted chestnuts in the air, with Christmas carols resounding around every corner. Whether you're looking for the ideal handmade ornament or indulging in Salzburg's legendary **Mozartkugeln**, Christmas shopping in Salzburg is a once-in-a-lifetime event!

Best Christmas Markets for Unique Souvenirs

Salzburg's Christmas markets are filled with one-of-a-kind presents and treasures that cannot be found anywhere else. These festive bazaars are brimming with handcrafted decorations, beautiful wood carvings, and traditional Austrian crafts that capture the spirit of the season.

Christkindlmarkt on Residenzplatz: This historic market is the hub of Salzburg's

Christmas retail scene. Wander among the quaint kiosks, where you can find anything from exquisite glass ornaments to scented candles and hand-knit scarves. Whether you're looking for a little present for a friend or a treasured souvenir for yourself, the Christkindlmarkt has plenty of alternatives for thoughtful gifts.

Stern Advent Market in Sternbräu: The Stern Advent Market offers a more intimate, tucked-away experience. Nestled in a courtyard, it's the ideal place to discover handmade products and handcrafted things. Consider handcrafted jewelry, embroidered linens, and unique toys for children. Plus, you can have a cup of **Glühwein** while browsing—it's all part of the experience!

Hellbrunner Adventzauber: If you want to experience something genuinely spectacular, the Christmas market at **Hellbrunn Palac**e is a must-see. Surrounded by the grandeur of the palace, this market sells local handicrafts with a festive flare. You may discover elaborate Christmas decorations, carved wooden figurines, and even traditional Austrian treats to take home. It's the kind of shop where each present tells a narrative about Salzburg's vibrant Christmas customs.

Boutiques and local shops with a Christmas twist.

While the markets get much of the attention, Salzburg's shops and small retailers also get into the festive mood. Many are dressed up in seasonal décor, creating a pleasant and welcoming environment for finding the right Christmas present.

Sporer Schnaps Boutique: This lovely business is ideal for anybody searching for one-of-a-kind, locally crafted spirits. Sporer Schnaps, with a history reaching back to 1903, provides a diverse assortment of schnapps and liqueurs, all of which make excellent presents. For an added festive touch, get a bottle of their limited-edition Christmas blend—it's the ideal holiday treat!

Christmas in Salzburg: This business specializes in all things Christmas and is open all year, but it is particularly spectacular around the holidays. From handmade decorations to traditional advent wreaths, you'll discover everything you need to inject some Salzburg flare into your Christmas décor.

It's a must-see if you want to capture a bit of Salzburg's festive enchantment.

Mozartkugeln and Other Salzburg Specialities

No Christmas shopping trip to Salzburg would be complete without purchasing some of the city's most recognized delicacies. These delectable delicacies are excellent stocking stuffers or hostess presents, and they provide a real flavor of Salzburg.

Mozartkugeln: These legendary chocolates are as fundamental to Salzburg's character as Mozart himself! Mozartkugeln, wrapped in shimmering foil and stuffed with marzipan and pistachios, are popular souvenirs. Pick yourself a box or two—whether for yourself or as a special present, these small treats are a must-have.

Stiegl Beer: Give the beer fan in your life a present from Stiegl, Salzburg's historic brewery. Purchase a festive beer gift package, packed with a few seasonal beers. It's an ideal way to share a taste of Austria with friends and family back home.

Lebkuchen and Vanillekipferl: Traditional Austrian Christmas sweets such as Lebkuchen (spiced gingerbread) and Vanillekipferl (vanilla crescents) are another excellent way to bring Salzburg's festive mood into your house. Many local bakeries have elegantly wrapped assortments that are ideal for gifting—or snacking on the plane journey home!

High-End Shopping for the Holidays

For those searching for something a bit more opulent, Salzburg's high-end shops provide lots of beautiful selections. Salzburg's luxury retailers provide a wide range of Christmas gift ideas, from designer clothing to exquisite jewelry.

Getreidegasse: This popular shopping strip is loaded with high-end businesses that sell everything from designer apparel to luxury leather products. Premium Austrian fashion is available at stores such as **Ludwig Reiter** and **Steffl**, while worldwide luxury labels may be found snuggled amongst lovely cafés and ancient buildings. The seasonal window decorations alone are worth seeing!

Schatzhaus Salzburg: If you want to give a genuinely extravagant present, the Schatzhaus jewelry shop has a stunning collection of fine jewels. Whether it's a sparkling necklace or a beautiful watch, you'll find something to make your loved one shine this Christmas.

Shopping for Christmas presents in Salzburg is an enjoyable experience. There's no better location to locate the ideal Christmas gifts than here, with its charming markets, local shops, and gastronomic delights. Each store, stall, and sweet treat embodies Salzburg's enchantment, making Christmas shopping a unique joyful journey.

Day Trips From Salzburg

Salzburg is a mesmerizing location during the winter season, but the neighboring areas provide even more wonderful experiences that make for ideal day getaways. Whether you're drawn to snow-covered villages, old salt mines, or dazzling lakeside towns, there's an experience waiting just beyond Salzburg's boundaries. From the snowy vistas of Hallstatt to the festive charm of St. Wolfgang, let's look at the greatest day excursions from Salzburg this holiday season!

Exploring Hallstatt in Winter

A visit to **Hallstatt** is like walking into a winter fantasy. This UNESCO World Heritage hamlet, perched on the banks of Hallstätter See and surrounded by towering snow-dusted mountains, is stunningly gorgeous all year, but it is especially spectacular in the winter.

Winter Wonderland by the Lake: With the hamlet covered in snow, Hallstatt's lakefront backdrop becomes even more tranquil. Take a walk along the quiet promenade, where magnificent Alpine homes are decked with holiday decorations and icicles dangle from their eaves. The reflections of the snow-capped mountains on the motionless lake create an incredible scene.

The Salt Mine Experience: One of Hallstatt's most well-known attractions is the **Hallstatt Salt Mine**, the world's oldest salt mine. Even in the winter, the mine is available to guests, providing an exciting underground trip that leads you deep into the mountain. Slide down wooden slides, explore historic tunnels, and learn about the area's long history of salt mining. It's a one-of-a-kind excursion that will make your winter getaway more exciting.

Berchtesgaden Christmas Village & Salt Mine Tours

Berchtesgaden, located in the Bavarian Alps and only a short drive over the border into Germany, is a winter wonderland. It's the perfect place to spend a day of festive exploration and adventure, thanks to its quaint **Christmas town** and renowned **salt mine**.

Festive Atmosphere in the Christmas Village: The town of Berchtesgaden changes into a lovely Christmas hamlet throughout the holiday season, with dazzling lights, cozy kiosks, and a welcoming festive ambiance. The town square has a charming Christmas market where visitors may drink mulled wine, eat traditional Bavarian foods, and browse for handcrafted presents. The magnificent Alpine background adds to the enchanting atmosphere.

Exploring the Salt Mine: For those who like adventure, the **Berchtesgaden Salt Mine** is a must-see trip. Take a guided tour of the subterranean world of salt mining, which includes miner's slides, a boat trip over a lighted salt lake, and intriguing anecdotes about the region's history. It's an instructive but exhilarating activity that adds a new dimension to your winter day trip.

The Advent Magic of St.Wolfgang and St. Gilgen

The lakeside communities of St. Wolfgang and St. Gilgen on Wolfgangsee are among the most romantic spots for a winter day excursion from Salzburg. These villages come alive around Advent, with dazzling lights reflecting off the lake and festive marketplaces filled with the aroma of gingerbread and mulled wine.

St. Wolfgang Advent Market: The Christmas market in St. Wolfgang is a regional highlight, with wooden booths filled with local handicrafts, baked delicacies, and festive decorations. The town's gorgeous church, lit by candlelight, contributes to the tranquil and nostalgic atmosphere. Take a stroll around the lake and enjoy the soft light of floating lanterns?It's a really wonderful sight.

St. Gilgen's Baroque Beauty: Just a short boat trip away, **St. Gilgen** has its own unique appeal throughout the Christmas season. This hamlet, noted for its Baroque beauty, is converted into a winter paradise complete with vibrant Christmas decorations and bustling marketplaces. The Advent market at **Mozartplatz** combines traditional cuisine, local crafts, and live entertainment to bring the town's Christmas spirit to life.

A Winter Day at Bad Ischl

Bad Ischl is the ideal day trip location for anyone seeking history, tranquility, and winter beauty. This spa town, which was originally the summer home of Austrian nobility, takes on a calm and joyful atmosphere during the winter months.

Winter Stroll Through Imperial History: Start your day in Bad Ischl by visiting the Kaiservilla, the former home of Emperor Franz Joseph and Empress Elisabeth. In the winter, the villa is surrounded by snow-covered grounds, providing a tranquil and historic backdrop to explore. The town itself is full of stunning architecture and delightful streets to explore.

Relaxation at the Thermal Baths: After a morning of exploration, warm up at one of Bad Ischl's well-known thermal baths. The **Eurotherme Spa** is extremely popular, featuring heated indoor and outdoor pools overlooking the snow-capped Alps. It's an ideal opportunity to relax and rejuvenate before returning to Salzburg.

Festive Café Experience: Bad Ischl also has the famed **Cafe Zauner,** one of Austria's most popular pastry shops. Stop by for a piece of **Zaunerstollen** or a steaming cup of hot chocolate and enjoy the caf?'s beautiful, old-world charm.

Salzburg may be your home base for a lovely winter holiday, but these adjacent places provide even more options for festive fun.

Whether you're seeing the icy beauty of Hallstatt, learning about St. Wolfgang's winter customs, or relaxing at a spa in Bad Ischl, these day excursions will add a magical touch to your Christmas in Salzburg. Each one provides a distinct combination of history, culture, and winter beauty, making them ideal compliments to your vacation schedule!

Sustainable & Eco-Friendly Winter Travel

As more tourists become conscious of their environmental effect, selecting sustainable and eco-friendly solutions has become a critical component of holiday planning. Salzburg, with its rich cultural heritage and breathtaking natural surroundings, is a city dedicated to conserving its beauty for future generations. During the festive winter season, there are several opportunities to enjoy Salzburg while making ethical decisions that lower your carbon impact and benefit the local community. Let's look at how you might celebrate a more sustainable and environmentally conscientious Christmas in Salzburg.

Eco-Friendly Accommodations and Practices

When planning a winter vacation to Salzburg, staying in eco-friendly lodgings is a simple yet effective approach to practice responsible travel. Fortunately, Salzburg has embraced green tourism, with several hotels, guesthouses, and inns undertaking environmentally friendly programs.

Certified Eco-Hotels: Look for lodgings with certificates such as the Austrian Ecolabel, which confirms that the hotel adheres to ecologically responsible practices. These eco-hotels utilize energy-efficient technology, minimize trash, and provide organic, locally produced cuisine. By staying at one of these accredited hotels, you directly support companies that promote sustainability.

Sustainable Practices in Hotels: Even if your hotel does not have an eco-certification, many Salzburg lodgings provide green options like towel and linen reuse programs, energy-efficient lighting, and water conservation measures. Be cautious of how you use resources throughout your stay?Turn off lights and heating when you leave your room, and avoid using towels or other amenities that you do not need.

Sustainable Holiday Shopping in Salzburg

One of the highlights of visiting Salzburg during the holidays is the opportunity to browse for unique presents in the city's many markets and shops. However, it is feasible to enjoy Christmas shopping while being cognizant of your environmental impact. Here are some suggestions for making your shopping experience more sustainable.

Support Local craftsmen: Salzburg's Christmas markets are brimming with handmade gifts created by local craftsmen. Whether it's a hand-carved wooden decoration or traditional Austrian jewelry, these items often have a smaller environmental effect than mass-produced counterparts. Buying from local producers helps the community and promotes traditional workmanship.

Choose Eco-Friendly and Reusable Gifts: As you browse the booths, search for presents manufactured from sustainable materials such as organic cotton, recycled textiles, or natural wood. Reusable products such as eco-friendly shopping bags, reusable water bottles, and bamboo cutlery offer lovely presents while also encouraging sustainability.

Choose minimum Packaging: When shopping presents, strive to choose things with minimum or eco-friendly packaging. Many local sellers utilize biodegradable or recyclable materials, which makes it easy to limit trash when Christmas shopping.

Winter Hiking and Responsible Outdoor Adventure

Salzburg is surrounded by stunning natural surroundings, and winter is the ideal season to explore these snowy panoramas via hiking and outdoor activities. However, it is important to participate in these activities appropriately, so that your pleasure of nature does not affect the ecosystem.

Stay On Designated Trails: Winter hiking in Salzburg provides stunning vistas of snow-covered mountains and woodlands. To maintain the natural environment, always follow identified trails and routes. This serves to avoid erosion and harm to the surrounding flora and wildlife, particularly during the harsh winter months.

Leave No Trace: When hiking, sledding, or just enjoying nature, observe the "Leave No Trace" guidelines. Pack up your waste, avoid disturbing animals, and resist the impulse to collect natural keepsakes. By conserving the natural environment, you help to preserve its beauty for future visitors.

Eco-Friendly Equipment: If you're planning an outdoor trip like skiing or snowshoeing, consider renting or purchasing used equipment. Many outdoor rental stores in Salzburg provide ecologically sourced or energy-efficient equipment, therefore lowering the environmental effect of your activities.

Salzburg's Commitment to Green Travel During Christmas

Salzburg is making great progress toward becoming a more sustainable city, with efforts focusing on green energy, trash reduction, and sustainable tourism practices, particularly during the peak holiday season.

Public Transportation & Low-Emission Travel: Salzburg's superb public transportation system employs sustainable energy, including electric buses and trains that link the city to its surroundings. During your visit, take use of these eco-friendly solutions rather than depending on private vehicles. The city also encourages bicycle riding, especially in the winter, by providing dedicated bike lanes and rental choices.

Christmas Market Initiatives: Many Salzburg Christmas markets have included environmentally friendly methods, such as utilizing reusable mugs for gluhwein (mulled wine) and providing locally produced organic cuisine. Vendors are also urged to decrease trash by using minimal packaging and providing biodegradable alternatives.

Energy-Efficient Christmas Decorations: Although Salzburg is known for its magnificent Christmas lights, the city is working to reduce its energy use. Many Christmas lights and decorations employ energy-efficient LED bulbs, which considerably reduces the environmental effect of the festive displays.

Salzburg is an amazing example of how a city can celebrate the festive season while remaining committed to sustainability. From eco-friendly hotels to careful Christmas shopping and responsible outdoor excursions, there are several ways to have a fun and memorable winter vacation in Salzburg while also helping the environment. By making minor adjustments to your travel patterns, you can help to create a greener, more sustainable future, ensuring that the charm of Salzburg's Christmas season is maintained for future generations.

Salzburg Christmas Traditions & Folklore

Salzburg during Christmas Time is more than simply a stunning background of glittering lights and snow-dusted roofs; it's a city where deep-rooted traditions and folklore bring the holiday season to life in ways that move the soul. The myths, traditions, and practices that have molded this city's holiday festivities for centuries lend levels of romance and mystery to each corner. From touching hymns to spine-tingling folklore, let's explore the distinctive customs that make Christmas in Salzburg really special.

The Story of Silent Night and Its Salzburg Roots

Perhaps no Christmas song is more popular than Silent Night (Stille Nacht), and its roots are strongly rooted in the Salzburg area. Joseph Mohr, a young priest, wrote this simple but powerful hymn in 1818 and put it to music by Franz Xaver Gruber, a schoolteacher. It was originally sung in the little community of Oberndorf, just north of Salzburg.

The carol was written at a difficult period in life. Mohr wrote the lyrics as poetry, seeking optimism in the aftermath of war and starvation. When the church organ failed soon before Christmas, Gruber improvised a piece for guitar. On Christmas Eve, the world heard Silent Night for the first time.

Visitors may now experience the wonder of this carol by visiting Oberndorf's Silent Night Chapel, which serves as a memorial to the song's birth. The song's message of peace and togetherness pervades Salzburg's Christmas festivities, and hearing it sung live in one of the city's old churches is an extraordinary experience that captures the genuine spirit of the season.

The Krampuslauf: A Chilling Christmas Tradition

While Salzburg's Christmas markets and performances are festive, there is a darker, more exhilarating aspect to the Austrian holiday season: the Krampuslauf. The Krampus, a terrifying demon from Alpine tradition, is reported to accompany Saint Nicholas, punishing mischievous youngsters with chains and birch rods.

Every December, the *Krampuslauf*, or *Krampus run*, takes place in Salzburg's streets, with individuals costumed in extravagant, horrifying costumes parading around town. These ghastly people, with fanged masks and monster horns, assault the streets in a chaotic yet interesting display. It's exhilarating and a touch creepy, but it's an important part of the local Christmas tradition.

The Krampus tradition extends back centuries and combines pre-Christian pagan practices with Christian Christmas festivities. Today, it is a popular event that adds excitement and a touch of dread to Salzburg's normally tranquil winter ambiance. If you're feeling courageous, joining the masses to see the Krampus run is an unforgettable experience!

Austrian Christmas Folklore And Legends

Austria is rich in tradition, and the Christmas season brings many of its myths and legends to life. Aside from Krampus, other characters such as Perchta?a mysterious, witch-like entity who was thought to reward the virtuous and punish the lazy?add to the mystery of Salzburg's Christmas festivities. Perchta, according to legend, would visit households throughout the twelve days of Christmas, praising those who performed domestic responsibilities but inflicting misery on those who did not.

Saint Nicholas (Nikolaus), another well-known character in Austrian mythology, pays visits to youngsters on December 6th and rewards them with sweets and little presents for good behavior. Saint Nicholas, unlike the Santa Claus character common to many countries, is a more traditional and serious figure clad in bishop's robes, and his visits are sometimes timed to coincide with joyful parades.

These folklore and myths imbue Salzburg's Christmas season with mystery and magic. Listening to local legends by the fire while sipping a cup of hot mulled wine allows you to experience the centuries-old traditions that still run through the city.

Festive Customs and How to Celebrate Like a Local

If you want to spend Christmas like a real Salzburger, you must adopt the city's lovely customs and joyful traditions. One of the most popular traditions is going to a midnight service on Christmas Eve, when melodies fill the air and the joyful message of the season is presented. Many people also assemble with their families to spend a peaceful evening at home, burning candles on their Christmas trees and sharing little presents.

Another highlight is the traditional Austrian Christmas supper, which usually includes delicacies like roast goose, carp, or turkey, as well as excellent side dishes like Kartoffelsalat (potato salad) or red cabbage. After supper, families share sweet snacks such as Vanillekipferl (vanilla crescent biscuits) and drink Gluhwein (mulled wine) to stay warm.

For visitors visiting Salzburg, participating in these local rituals is an excellent opportunity to experience the genuine flavor of an Austrian Christmas. Whether you're eating festive delicacies, listening to live Christmas music, or participating in local holiday festivities, you'll immediately feel like a member of the community as you absorb the warmth and excitement of Salzburg's seasonal traditions.

Salzburg's Christmas customs and culture are what make the city's holiday season so special. From the terrifying Krampus to the calming sounds of Silent Night, each tale and custom lends depth and character to the festive season. Whether you're here to learn about history or have fun, Salzburg's Christmas atmosphere will leave you with memories that last a lifetime.

Practical Tips for Your Christmas Vacation

Planning a Christmas trip to Salzburg may be both thrilling and daunting, particularly given the city's popularity during the holiday season. Whether you're an experienced traveler or a first-time visitor, being well-prepared is essential for getting the most of your trip. This chapter contains crucial practical recommendations for packing for Salzburg's winter, managing the Christmas crowds, and ensuring your safety throughout your trip.

Packing for a Winter Trip to Salzburg

Salzburg's winter weather may be unpredictable, ranging from cool to downright freezing, with the rare snowfall. Packing adequately is essential for remaining comfortable when visiting the city's Christmas markets, historical sites, and outdoor activities. Here are some basics to add on your packing list.

Layered Clothing: Start with thermal base layers, then a warm sweater or fleece, and finish with a waterproof winter coat. Layering enables you to adapt to both indoor and outdoor temperatures.

Winter Accessories: Remember to bring a warm hat, scarf, gloves, and thick socks. These simple things may make a significant difference in keeping you warm on lengthy treks or during outdoor activities.

Waterproof Boots: In the winter, Salzburg's streets may become wet and slippery, so strong, waterproof boots with high traction are required. Choose walking boots if you want to explore the city on foot.

Reusable Water Bottle: Staying hydrated is as vital in winter as it is in summer. Bring a reusable water bottle to refill during the day.

Travel-Sized Toiletries: If you intend on attending any Christmas festivities or concerts, bring a few compact toiletries, such as hand sanitizer or a travel comb, to freshen up.

Weather Conditions and How To Prepare

Salzburg in December is wonderful, but the cold weather necessitates careful preparation. Average temperatures vary from -2°C to 5°C

(28°F to 41°F), and snowfall is widespread, resulting in a stunning winter wonderland. Here are some suggestions to help you prepare for Salzburg's winter weather:

Check the forecast: Before you go, look at the weather prediction for Salzburg. While it is normal to have cold and snowy weather, there may also be rain or warmer temperatures. Being prepared for both can help you pack properly.

Prepare for snow: Snowy days are common in December, which means sidewalks and roadways may become ice. If you want to walk a lot, pack snow grips for your shoes or buy boots with non-slip soles.

Protect your Electronics: Cold weather may drain batteries quicker than normal, so keep your phone and camera close to your body to extend their life. Consider taking a portable charger, particularly if you expect to be gone all day.

Navigating Christmas Crowds and Tourist Tips

Salzburg is a renowned Christmas destination, and the holiday season attracts visitors from all over the globe. While crowds contribute to the festive mood, they may make traversing the city more difficult. Here is how to manage:

Plan Early: If you want to attend any popular events, such as Christmas concerts or special holiday meals, make your tickets or reservations as soon as possible. Many events sell out rapidly, particularly in December.

Visit Markets Early or Late: The Christmas markets may be quite packed, especially in the late afternoon and early evening. To escape the biggest crowds, go to the markets early in the morning when they first open or late in the evening after the dinner rush.

Explore Beyond the City Center: While the major markets and sights are in the center of Salzburg, try visiting less-crowded locations like the Hellbrunn Christmas Market. You'll still enjoy the holiday mood, just with fewer people.

Be Patient and Flexible: With an increase in visitors, anticipate some delays, particularly in popular areas such as restaurants and during peak hours at markets. Being patient and flexible with your schedule will allow you to enjoy the trip without undue worry.

Salzburg Winter Safety and Emergency Contacts

Ensuring your safety during your Salzburg Christmas holiday is critical, particularly in winter when ice conditions and freezing temperatures may be challenging.

Be Wary of Ice: Snow and ice may make roads and walkways treacherous. Walk cautiously, particularly on cobblestone streets, and utilize handrails if available. If you're going into more rural or steep locations, carry trekking poles for extra stability.

Stay Warm: Frostbite and hypothermia are serious risks in cold weather, particularly if you're spending a lengthy time outdoors. Take frequent stops inside to warm up and sip hot drinks like as *Glühwein* or tea.

Know Emergency Contacts: Keep a list of local emergency contacts nearby, such as:

- *European Emergency Number (112):* Used across the EU for police, medical, and fire emergencies.

- *Salzburg Tourist Information:* For help navigating the city or locating specialized services.
- *Pharmacies:* Many pharmacies in Salzburg provide 24-hour service over the holiday season, making them an excellent resource for any medical issues.

Following these practical tips will ensure that you are well-prepared to appreciate all Salzburg has to offer over the Christmas season. Whether you're traversing the seasonal markets or relaxing in a classic café, learning how to deal with the cold and crowds can help you make the most of your trip.

Conclusion

Salzburg during Christmas is like a living fairy tale. Its combination of historical charm, festive customs, and magnificent winter landscape makes it a popular choice for those looking for a spectacular Christmas experience. From the legendary Christmas markets that fill the city's squares with dazzling lights and wonderful fragrances to the world-class performances and activities that commemorate the season, Salzburg has something for everyone during this special time of year.

As you've seen in this book, Salzburg offers several possibilities to get into the festive mood. Whether you're admiring the snow-covered roofs from the Hohensalzburg Fortress, eating a classic Austrian meal at one of the city's quaint restaurants, or ice skating at Mozartplatz, the city welcomes you to make memorable memories. The mix of cultural events, such as attending a classical Mozart performance, and adventurous sports, such as skiing or sledding, makes this a perfect location for all sorts of tourists, from families and couples to single adventurers.

Furthermore, Salzburg's rich traditions, such as the terrifying Krampuslauf and the narrative of "Silent Night," enable tourists to engage with centuries-old rituals that distinguish the city's Christmas celebration. These materials evoke a strong feeling of nostalgia and warmth, reminding us of the delight of spending time with loved ones throughout the holidays.

Salzburg, with its physical beauty, cultural depth, and festive spirit, embodies the true charm of Christmas. Whether you spend your time shopping for unique presents, indulging in local specialties, or discovering the city's hidden secrets, Salzburg's winter splendor will make an indelible impression. As you think on your vacation, you'll definitely be motivated to return, knowing that the allure of Salzburg during Christmas is an experience worth revisiting every year.

Printed in Great Britain
by Amazon